CONTENTS

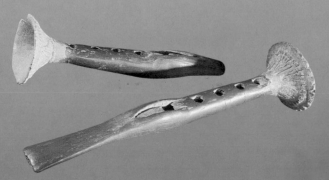

◀Aztec pottery flutes, played at feasts and festivals.

MEET THE AZTECS

Savages, killers, beggars, strangers – these were just some of the names people called the Aztecs when they first arrived in Mesoamerica. That was around AD 1200. But just 300 years later, the Aztecs controlled almost all the region.

Originally, the Aztec people lived in North America. They were farmers and warriors. But, mysteriously, they had to leave their homeland. This may have been because of climate change. Probably, the Aztecs ran short of water and their crops died. So, led by priests carrying a statue of their tribal god, Huitzilopochtli (say 'hweet-sil-oh-pok-tlee'), they headed south, looking for a new home.

Mesoamerica. The shaded area shows the land where the Aztecs lived. They called it 'Anahuac', which means 'the land between the waters'. Today, its name is Mexico.

▼ *This pyramid-tomb, with a temple to the gods on top, was built by the Maya people between AD 550–900.*

STRANGE HISTORIES
THE AZTECS

Fiona Macdonald

Chrysalis Children's Books

LOOK FOR THE AZTEC

Look for the Aztec in boxes like this. Here you will find extra facts, stories and other interesting information about the strange world of the Aztecs.

First published in the UK in 2003 by
Chrysalis Children's Books
An imprint of Chrysalis Books Group Plc
The Chrysalis Building, Bramley Road,
London W10 6SP

Paperback edition first published in 2005
Copyright © Chrysalis Books Group Plc 2003

Produced by
Monkey Puzzle Media Ltd
Gissing's Farm, Fressingfield
Suffolk IP21 5SH, UK

Designer: Jamie Asher
Editor: Kate Phelps
Picture Research: Lynda Lines

ISBN 1 84138 667 7 (hb)
ISBN 1 84458 251 5 (pb)

British Library Cataloguing in Publication Data for this book is available from the British Library.

Printed in China
10 9 8 7 6 5 4 3 2 1

Acknowledgements
We wish to thank the following individuals and organizations for their help and assistance and for supplying material in their collections: AKG front cover and back cover left 6 bottom, 22 top, 24 top; Ancient Art and Architecture Collection back cover right, 8 bottom (Ronald Sheridan), 9 (Haruko/Sheridan), 11 top (Haruko/Sheridan), 20 top (Ronald Sheridan), 23 top, 27, 28; Art Archive 8 top (Pitti Palace, Florence/ Dagli Orti), 17 top, 18 top (Museo del Templo Mayor, Mexico/Dagli Orti), 19 (National Archives, Mexico/Mireille Vautier), 21 (Museo de America, Madrid/Dagli Orti), 30 (Museum für Volkerkunde, Vienna); Bodleian Library, Oxford University 12 both; Corbis 1 (Gianni Dagli Orti), 6 top (Gianni Dagli Orti), 7 (Gianni Dagli Orti), 13 (Richard A Cooke), 14 (Bettmann), 15 both (Bettmann), 17 bottom (Bettmann), 25 top (Historical Picture Archive), 25 bottom (Gianni Dagli Orti), 29 (Bettmann); Topham Picturepoint 20 bottom, 23 bottom; Werner Forman Archive 2 (Museum für Volkerkunde, Vienna), 3 (British Museum, London), 4 bottom, 5, 10 (National Museum of Anthropology, Mexico City), 11 middle (British Museum, London), 16 (National Museum of Anthropology, Mexico City), 18 bottom (British Musum, London), 22 bottom (Museum für Volkerkunde, Vienna), 26 (Liverpool Museum). Artwork by Michael Posen.

◄ *An Aztec army commander (right) giving orders to a conquered enemy.*

When the Aztecs arrived in Mesoamerica, they found it was already very full! For over 2000 years, the region had been home to many splendid civilizations, including the Olmecs, the Maya and the Toltecs. Many smaller groups of people also lived there. Each civilization had its own language, laws, customs and skills, but they also shared many traditions.

The Aztecs were crafty and very clever. They quickly learned what they could from Mesoamerican peoples, but kept all their own ancient laws and customs as well. This meant they had lots of wisdom, knowledge and practical experience to help them to survive.

AZTEC WORDS

The Aztecs spoke *Nahuatl* (say 'nah-hwat-ull'). It was related to several Native North American languages and quite different from most others spoken in the land where they settled. In Nahuatl, the Aztecs' name for themselves was 'Mexica' (say 'mesh-ee-ca'). Today, this has become the name of a nation, Mexico.

▶ *These carved stone warriors, over 5m tall, were built to hold up the roof of a temple built by the Toltec people, around AD 800.*

THE CITY IN THE LAKE

When the Aztecs first arrived in Mesoamerica, they were definitely not welcome. But they were determined to stay. They dreamt their god had sent a sign to guide them to a new home and they must build a city where they saw an eagle eating a snake, sitting in a prickly-pear cactus.

So they travelled on, searching for the dream sign. Finally they found it, around AD 1325. But it was on a barren island, crawling with snakes, in the middle of a swampy lake in the deep Central Valley of Mexico. Close by, volcanoes released clouds of poisonous gas. How could anyone make a home there?

▲ *This Aztec drawing shows the name of their capital city, Tenochtitlán, in picture-writing.*

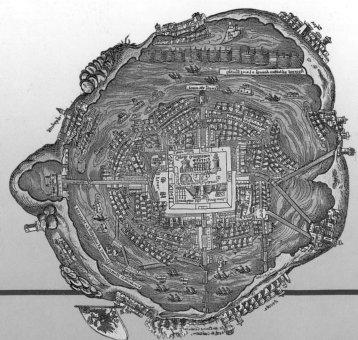

▶ *The Aztecs' capital city of Tenochtitlán, portrayed by Spanish explorers in 1524. You can see the houses packed close together on the island in the middle of the lake.*

The Aztecs were sure they would survive. To them, this unpromising site was the centre of the universe and Aztec people were brave as well as determined. They killed the snakes and ate them and built houses and temples on the island. They gave their city a name, Tenochtitlán (say tay-nok-teet-lan), which means Place of the Prickly Pear. There was no space on the island to grow food, so Aztec farmers built *chinampas* (say chee-nam-pas), or floating farms, all around it, in the lake.

Aztec architects designed a huge aqueduct to bring fresh water to the city from mountain streams and built raised walkways across the shallow lake. These linked the island to the surrounding shore. By 1500, Tenochtitlán was one of the biggest cities in the world.

▲ *Chinampas were made of reeds and rushes, piled high with earth and weighed down with stones.*

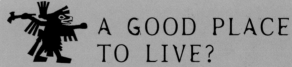 A GOOD PLACE TO LIVE?

The Aztecs' city was not a healthy place to live. Its climate was harsh, with droughts and heatwaves. There were also poisonous plants and spiders, and the threat of earthquakes. Killer germs and mosquitoes bred in the lake, which slowly grew salty and slimy, as its water evaporated.

GREAT SPEAKER

The Aztecs had two rulers: a king, called Tlatoani (say 'tlah-twa-nee'), or Great Speaker, and his deputy, Cihuacoatl (say 'si-hwa-ko-at-ull'), or Snake Woman. No one is quite sure why, since Snake Woman was always a man! To begin with, the Great Speaker was elected but soon, the position was taken over by one family, who passed it from father to son.

The Great Speaker was served by hundreds of officials, including priests, army commanders, judges, tax collectors, market overseers, scribes and spies. Many nobles (families descended from the first Aztec king) also served as royal advisors. They all went to the royal palace to receive orders. This was a vast building, with huge rooms (one could seat 3000 people), set in beautiful gardens with fountains and pools. Below the king, priests and nobles, there were several less powerful groups in Aztec society.

▲ *The Great Speaker was honoured almost like a god. When he left the royal palace, his feet were not allowed to touch the ground. So he was carried shoulder-high on a litter, or stood on special mats.*

► *Noble warriors and priests making offerings to the gods.*

Ordinary families were farmers, craftworkers, travelling merchants and market traders. They were organized into *calpulli* (say 'cal-pool-ee') or clans. Each clan owned land, which was shared. Clans were responsible for members' good behaviour and sometimes ran schools for their children. Rank and riches were usually decided by birth.

But a brave warrior could rise to become very respected. There were also many slaves – prisoners captured in battle, criminals or poor people who had sold themselves to get money for food.

▲ *Aztec merchants and craftworkers. Merchants, called* pochteca *(say 'pok-tay-ca'), travelled long distances, buying and selling. They joined together in a secret society and often acted as government spies!*

 AZTEC LAWS

All Aztec people had to obey strict laws. The punishments for breaking them could be very severe. The higher a person's rank, the worse their punishment. A judge or noble could be killed for being drunk in public, but an ordinary person might only have their head shaved (a sign of shame) for a first offence.

FOOD AND DRINK

The Aztecs ate mostly maize (sweetcorn). Aztec women ground dry maize grains on flat stones to make flour. They mixed this with water, shaped the dough into balls and rolled them out. Then they baked them on a hot clay dish to make crispy tortillas or wrapped them round a meat or vegetable mixture and steamed them to make pancakes.

Aztec cooks, always women, also made porridge from maize grains or from the seeds of sage and other wild plants. For extra nourishment, and to add flavour, they served up almost anything edible they could find. Mostly, they made spicy vegetable stews, with chillies, tomatoes, beans, pumpkins, sweet potatoes, peppers, avocados and boiled cactus leaves, with the spines removed. Luxury foods included meat such as rabbit, deer, turkey and hairless dog.

▼ *This museum model shows Aztec people buying and selling food in the market.*

◄ An Aztec food for special occasions – hairless dog!

► Rich Aztecs served food and drink from decorated pottery, like these tall cups (left) and bowl (right).

The Aztecs themselves did not have cheese, milk or butter; there were no cows, sheep, goats or horses in Mesoamerica. They didn't have sugar, either, but they did collect honey from wild bees. They drank water or tea made with dried herbs and also brewed beer from chewed maize. Aztec kings, rich nobles and merchants could afford a very special drink, called *xocolatl* (say 'sho-kol-at-ull'), or chocolate made from crushed cacao beans, honey and spices.

CACTUS POWER

The Aztecs brewed a strong alcoholic drink, called *pulque* (say 'pul-kay'), from maguey cactus sap or boiled it to make sticky syrup for sweetening food. They also found many strange uses for other parts of the plant. Its sharp spines were used like knives to draw blood in religious rituals. The pointed tips of its leaves could even be cut off and, with a long length of fibre attached, served as an instant needle and thread.

FAMILY LIFE

All Aztecs expected to get married. It was difficult for anyone to survive without a large family to support them. Families worked together, in businesses or on farms. They helped and looked after each other, too. If one member behaved badly, the whole family might be punished.

Old people, that is, anyone over 40, were respected for their knowledge and experience. They were given special privileges by Aztec laws. At wedding feasts, they were allowed to get drunk. Boys usually got married when they were about 20 years old, and girls when they were about 16. Marriages were arranged by matchmakers or families. It was rude for a girl to say 'yes' the first time she was asked!

▲ *Drinking at an Aztec feast. The people sitting down are old men and women. They are drunk, while the younger people, who are standing, watch over them.*

▼ *When an Aztec bride arrived at her groom's family home, she was led to sit on a mat by the hearth. The groom sat beside her and their clothes were knotted together as a sign they were wed.*

An Aztec wedding was an important event. The bride painted her face red or yellow and put on garlands of feathers and flowers. Then she was carried on the matchmaker's back to her bridegroom's parents' house. That would be her home for the rest of her life. Like most Aztec houses, it was small, plain and simple, made of mud brick or soft stone, whitewashed and thatched with reeds or cactus leaves. There was very little furniture, just a few mats, blankets, baskets and clay cooking pots. The Aztecs did not have tables, chairs, beds or metal tools.

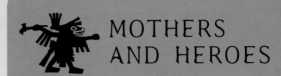

MOTHERS AND HEROES

Childbirth was the most dangerous time in any married woman's life. Although friends and midwives offered careful advice, such as 'don't go out at night for fear of evil spirits', many mothers died. The Aztecs honoured these dead women like gods or heroes and believed that their bodies had magic powers. Warriors tried to steal their hair or fingers as good-luck charms to hang on their shields.

▶ *This clay model shows four Aztec houses, with women working in the courtyards outside each one.*

GROWING UP

Aztec parents loved their children. They gave them affectionate nicknames, such as Precious Feather or Jewel, and cared for them very well. Strict Aztec laws meant that a father could be punished if he did not work hard to support his family.

Newborn babies were welcomed into the world with cries of joy. Family members ran around, shouting the new baby's name.

CHILDREN'S DUTIES

Children had to help around the home. By the time they were four, boys were expected to fetch water and carry firewood. When they were six, they began to learn how to work in the fields. Girls aged 12 were taught cooking, and boys aged 13 were taught how to paddle and steer a canoe.

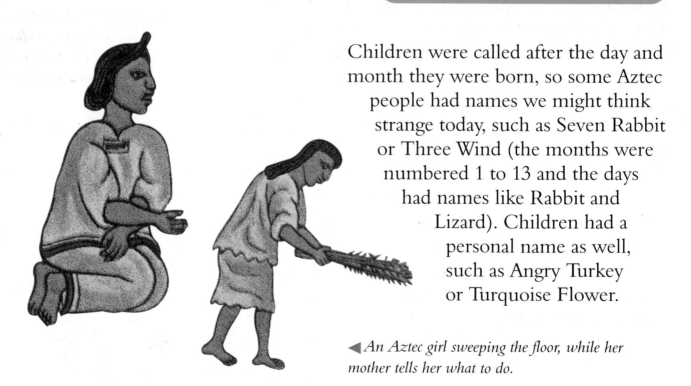

Children were called after the day and month they were born, so some Aztec people had names we might think strange today, such as Seven Rabbit or Three Wind (the months were numbered 1 to 13 and the days had names like Rabbit and Lizard). Children had a personal name as well, such as Angry Turkey or Turquoise Flower.

◀ *An Aztec girl sweeping the floor, while her mother tells her what to do.*

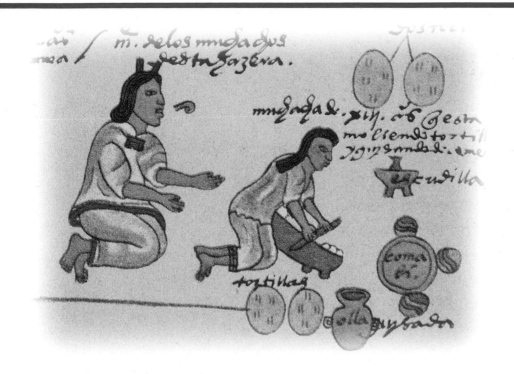

◀ *Making tortillas. Aztec parents carefully controlled the amount their children ate, according to their age. At 14, they were allowed two tortillas per day, plus vegetables.*

As they grew up, boys and girls were taught to be respectful, obedient and cheerful. Aztec children enjoyed lots of toys and games, and teenage girls sometimes challenged local boys to pillow fights. But if children were rude or lazy, their parents could punish them. They might be shut outside overnight or pricked with cactus spikes.

Girls stayed at home and were taught household skills by their mothers. Boys from ordinary families learned to be craftworkers, labourers or farmers. At 15, most boys went to local schools to learn to be warriors. Boys from rich or noble families might train to be priests or scribes. They studied history, astronomy and poetry, and were taught how to read and write.

▼ *The worst Aztec punishment for a child was to hold him or her over a fire of burning chillies. The smoke made their eyes, throats and lungs sting, which was very painful. (Do not burn chillies: it could be dangerous).*

LOOKING GOOD

The Aztecs did not follow fashion. Whatever their age, rank or the time of year, the basic design of their clothes stayed the same. Men and boys wore a loincloth and a short blanket tied at one shoulder to make a cloak. Women and girls wore a loose blouse and an ankle-length skirt.

By law, ordinary people's clothes had to be made of plain material. Usually this was made of cactus fibre. It was rough and coarse, but not prickly. Nobles were allowed to wear finer, smoother cloth, woven from cotton and decorated with brightly coloured embroidery. It was a serious crime for an ordinary person to dress in nobles' clothes. If found out, the person might be executed.

Noblewomen and noblemen were also allowed to wear jewellery and headdresses made with the beautiful feathers of rare rainforest birds. They could also carry fans and flowers. Aztec jewellery was carefully made by hand from pure gold, precious stones, coral, pearls and jade.

▲ *This gold nose-ornament was made by the Mixtec people of Mesoamerica for an Aztec noble to wear.*

 GET WEAVING

Cloth was woven by women and girls using backstrap looms. These were light and portable and could be used almost anywhere. Aztec weavers used this simple technology to create very complicated patterns based on shells, jewels, fish, monsters, jaguars and butterflies.

You could tell a lot about an Aztec by looking at his or her hairstyle. Young girls wore their hair long and loose. Young men, who had not yet killed an enemy in battle, did so as well. They had to leave some of their hair uncut to show that they were not yet 'real men'. Married women braided their hair and arranged it in two horns on top of their head. Adult warriors cut their hair at about ear-length and tied some of it up in a topknot.

▶ *An Aztec noblewoman (at the front of the picture) cooks food for two noble guests.*

▼ *A backstrap loom (below right). Aztec women and girls often wove feathers, shells and glittering wings from tropical beetles into the cloth, to make extra-beautiful designs.*

GODS AND FESTIVALS

Religion was a powerful force in Aztec peoples' lives. It affected everything they did: working, playing, fighting and even getting up in the morning. First thing every day, Aztec men, women and children pricked their ears and offered two drops of blood to the gods to give thanks for still being alive.

Most Aztecs worshipped many different gods and goddesses. Each one had different powers. Some were the spirits of dead rulers, who guided their descendants. Some were ancient nature gods, honoured by all Mesoamerican peoples. Some, like Huitzilopochtli, or God of the Sun, belonged to the Aztecs alone. But a few Aztecs preferred to worship just one supreme god. They called him Tloque Nahuaque (say 'tlow-kay nah-hwah-kay'), or Lord of Nowhere, because he was everywhere.

▲ *Aztec images of their gods could be fearsome, like this carved stone head of Tlaloc (say 'tlah-loke'), the rain-god.*

▶ *The Aztecs liked music with a strong rhythmic beat for dancing at festivals. Skilled musicians played the* teponaztli, *or two-note drum. Young people joined in on pottery flutes (right), whistles and ocarinas.*

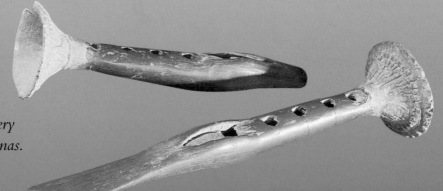

18

THE AZTEC BALL GAME

This game was played by two teams on a stone court about 60m long by 10m wide. Players tried to hit a solid rubber ball through stone rings placed high on the court's walls, using only their upper arms, hips and knees. Play was fierce, and injuries were common. Winners received rich prizes, but losers might be killed as offerings to the gods. The ball game was the Aztecs' favourite sport but it also had a religious meaning. The movements of the ball were meant to encourage the Sun as it made its daily journey across the sky.

Gods could be kind, but the witches, ghosts and demons that haunted the night were all very dangerous. They appeared as skulls that chased passers-by, as spooky miniature women or as headless and footless creatures who moaned and rolled on the ground. Monsters called *tzitzimime* (say 'tsee-tsee-mee-may') who wore necklaces and headdresses of cut-off human hands also lay in wait, ready to pounce on their victims.

The Aztecs honoured their gods and kept ghosts and demons at bay by holding elaborate festivals. Some were violent and terrifying. Others were more cheerful, with music, singing and dancing in the streets, feasting and ritual games.

▶ *Most Aztec festivals included human sacrifice and even cannibalism! Only the arms and legs were eaten – and the palms of the hands. Here, a victim about to be killed is balanced on top of a tall pole.*

AZTEC TEMPLES

The Aztecs built temples as homes for their gods. The Great Temple that towered almost 30m high in the centre of Tenochtitlán was a symbol of Aztec pride. It housed statues of Huitzilopochtli, the Aztecs' own special god, and Tlaloc, the God of Rain.

Temples began as pyramid-shaped mounds made of earth, stones and cement. They grew taller over the years as each new king added an extra layer or built a new shrine (holy room) on top of the mound. Shrines were reached by dangerously steep steps, often too small to put a whole foot on. Priests kept constant vigil there, offering flowers, incense and prayers. They also drummed, chanted and made human sacrifices to the gods.

▲ *An Aztec warrior (left) captures a prisoner, who will later be killed as a sacrifice.*

▼ *No Aztec temples have survived. They were pulled down by Spanish conquerors. But we can get some idea of what they were like by looking at temples built by other Mesoamerican people. This is the Temple of the Sun, built by Maya people at Teotihuacán around AD 600.*

WHAT DID VICTIMS THINK ABOUT SACRIFICES?

Aztec priests and poets taught that it was an honour to be sacrificed, and there are few reports of victims protesting. But they may have been drugged or lulled into a trance by the priests' chanting and drumming. Or they may have agreed to die in the hope of a good life in the next world.

▲ *Priests cutting the hearts out of victims, while blood runs down the temple steps. Most temples also had a rack outside where thousands of victims skulls were displayed. In front of the temple, Aztec men and women offer prayers to the gods.*

The Aztecs believed that they must feed the gods with blood, human hearts or human tears, or the world would come to an end. To do this, they killed criminals and prisoners captured in war, usually by cutting their hearts out. Special sacrificial stones stood at the top of temple steps where priests killed victims with sharp flint knives. *Chac-mool* containers – shaped like water-gods – were placed nearby to hold the hearts, while blood poured down the temple steps.

The ideal victim was young, fit, handsome and, preferably, male. The Aztecs thought they should only give the best to the gods. Priests also drowned Aztec children in springtime to encourage the rain to fall and beheaded young girls (the same height as the tall maize plants) when the first maize-cobs were ready to harvest in the hope this would guarantee good crops.

AZTECS AT WAR

The Aztecs were fighters. They fought their way into Mexico and had to keep on fighting to survive. At first, their main task was to defend their city but they soon found they needed to conquer more land to find enough food to survive.

They did this by taking control of the city-states all around them. They sent armies to invade them or ambassadors to threaten an attack. Usually, city leaders surrendered, and the Aztec Empire grew rapidly after around AD 1400. Aztec armies did not destroy the cities they conquered: instead they collected tributes (taxes) from them twice a year. They demanded an extraordinary range of very valuable items, such as feathers, baskets of chillies, necklaces, lip plugs, jaguar skins, jade and turquoise, gold dust and cacao beans.

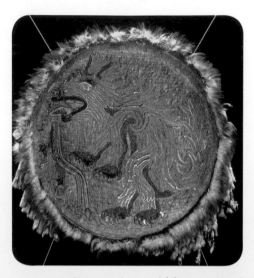

▲ Senior Aztec soldiers carried beautiful feather shields into battle. They believed they had magic, protective powers. This shield is decorated with a fierce coyote (a wild dog, rather like a wolf).

▲ Army commanders after a battle. The man on the right is giving orders. The man on the left is making a 'surrender' sign with his hand.

 TAKING PRISONERS

Strangely, the Aztecs did not aim to kill their opponents in battle. Instead, they hoped to capture them alive and take them back to their temples to be sacrificed to the gods. While an enemy prisoner was still alive, the Aztec who captured him was meant to treat him kindly, like a father, and feed him well.

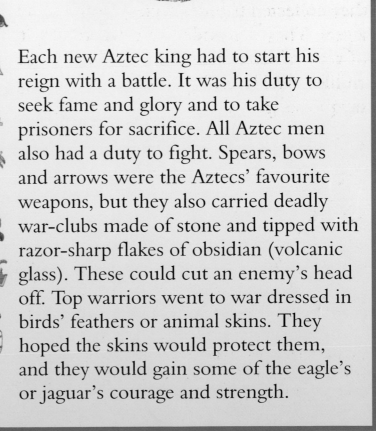

This Aztec stone carving portrays an 'eagle knight', a member of an elite fighting force who went into battle dressed in eagle skins.

A list in Aztec picture-writing, showing goods paid as tribute by conquered states. They include decorated blankets (to be worn as cloaks), baskets of chillies, and feathered shields.

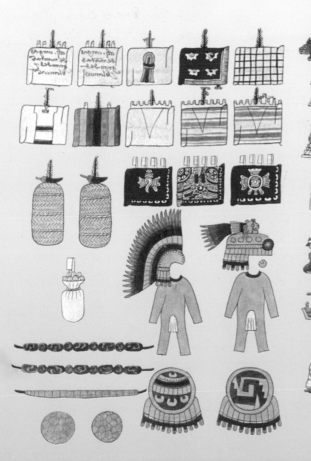

Each new Aztec king had to start his reign with a battle. It was his duty to seek fame and glory and to take prisoners for sacrifice. All Aztec men also had a duty to fight. Spears, bows and arrows were the Aztecs' favourite weapons, but they also carried deadly war-clubs made of stone and tipped with razor-sharp flakes of obsidian (volcanic glass). These could cut an enemy's head off. Top warriors went to war dressed in birds' feathers or animal skins. They hoped the skins would protect them, and they would gain some of the eagle's or jaguar's courage and strength.

THE END OF LIFE

Death was everywhere in the Aztec world – in wars, on long journeys, by sacrifice, through witchcraft or from illness. Many Aztec children died before they reached five years old, and most men and women died before they were 50.

Aztec medicine was a mixture of religion, herbalism, magic and first aid. Doctors set broken limbs expertly in plaster, cleaned wounds with urine (strangely, this was safer than dirty water), said prayers and recited magic spells. They grew herbs and medicinal plants in gardens and collected seeds and berries from wild rainforests. Some Aztec treatments worked, but others were very dangerous.

The bodies of important Aztecs were buried in tombs. They were dressed in fine clothes, and all their treasures were buried with them, together with a pet dog for company. If they were male, and really powerful, some of their wives and servants might be killed and buried, too.

▲ *Masks were used to cover the faces of the dead, and were also worn by priests in religious ceremonies. This mask, made of turquoise mosaic, shows the face of the god Quetzalcoatl (say 'kayt-sal-co-at-ull').*

FIFTH AND FINAL WORLD

The Aztecs' worst fear was that the world would come to an end. They believed it had been destroyed four times before, by jaguars, wind, fire and water. Each time, it had been born again. But now they lived in the fifth, and final, world. If it ended, there would be nothing at all.

Ordinary peoples' corpses were wrapped in cloth to make a mummy-bundle. This was decorated with paper ornaments and feathers, and a mask was placed over its face. Then the whole bundle was burnt.

Most Aztecs feared a miserable future after death. The Wind of Knives would cut the flesh from their bones, and they would spend four years on a dangerous journey, chased by monsters, until they reached *Mictlan* (say 'meek-tlan') – hell. Then they would disappear. But warriors, mothers who died in childbirth and human sacrifices would be reborn.

▲ *The Aztecs believed that steam and the scent of herbs could help drive out illness from the body. So they built mud-brick 'steam baths' to treat sick people.*

◄ *This carved stone calendar stood in the Aztecs' most important temple, in Tenochtitlán. It shows the sun-god, picture signs for days of the year, and images of the earthquake they believed would signal the end of the world. Aztec priests also used the calendar-stone to help them predict eclipses of the sun.*

Aztec Facts

Here is a selection of interesting facts about the strange world of the Aztecs.

Simple technology

The Aztecs had no iron, no roads, no horses, no big machines and no wheeled transport, though they did make wheeled toys.

Money beans

There were no coins or banknotes in Aztec lands. Instead, the Aztecs bartered (exchanged) goods of equal value and used cacao beans or quills filled with gold dust as money.

No recognition

Aztec artists and craftworkers did not sign their work. They believed their skills were a gift from the gods, so they did not deserve individual praise.

Bark books

Only specially trained scribes could read and write. A scribe, called a *tlacuilo* (say 'tlah-kweel-oh'), meaning 'thought-writer', would use picture writing to record Aztec history, myths and astronomy. Aztec books, called codexes, were made of long, folded strips of fig-tree bark or deerskin.

End of the world

Like many other Mesoamericans, the Aztecs worshipped Quetzalcoatl, or Feathered Serpent, an ancient god-king. They believed he had sacrificed himself to help the people he ruled. Legends told how, one day, he would return to Mexico. Soon afterwards, the world would end.

▼ *An Aztec codex (folding book).*

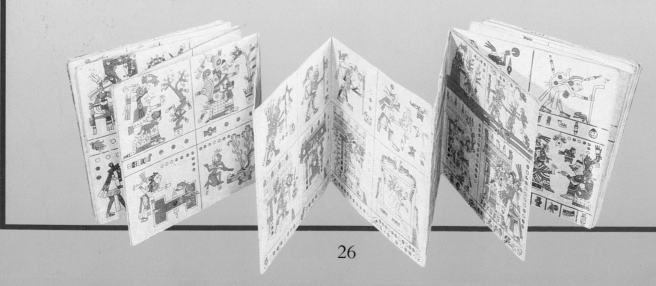

STRANGE MEN

In 1519, Spanish nobleman Hernan Cortés landed in Mexico with a troop of soldiers. They were searching for gold. The Aztecs had never seen European men before and were alarmed by their hairy chests and bushy beards. They thought that the new arrivals might be Quetzalcoatl or other strange, feathered gods. They were also puzzled by European sailing ships, which looked like huge houses, floating on the water, and by men riding on horseback. To the Aztecs, they seemed to be monsters, half human, half beast.

▶ *This modern mask was made to wear during celebrations of the Mexican Day of the Dead.*

ODD EVENTS

Shortly before Hernan Cortés and the Spanish landed, priests reported many strange omens. These included a temple catching fire, a tidal wave and weird, bodiless voices wailing in the streets at night.

END OF THE AZTECS

Cortés made friends with the Aztecs' enemies, and together they marched on Tenochtitlán. In 1521, Cortés and his soldiers set fire to the city and killed three-quarters of its people. Aztec power ended in 1524, when the last Aztec king died. In 1535, Mexico was made a colony, ruled by Spain, and many Spanish people migrated to live there.

AZTEC SURVIVORS

People descended from the Aztecs still live in Mexico today. They speak Nahuatl, the Aztec language, eat favourite Aztec foods and, sometimes, wear clothes with Aztec designs. Many Aztec customs also survive, mingled with Christian traditions. For example, on the Day of the Dead, Mexican families bring flowers and sweets shaped like Aztec-style skulls to their ancestors' graves.

AZTEC WORDS

This glossary explains some of the words used in this book that you might not have seen before.

Calpulli
Aztec family group, or clan. It kept law and order and provided schools and welfare benefits.

Chac-mool
A stone statue shaped like a river-god (or a dying warrior) holding a large dish. The dish was used to hold hearts from human sacrifices.

Cihuacoatl
Snake Woman, the Aztecs' deputy king.

City-state
A city and the land surrounding it.

Clan
A group of people descended from one ancestor, and their husbands, wives and children.

Codex
A folding book.

▼ *A stone chac-mool shaped like a river-god. It was used to collect human hearts during sacrifices.*

Herbalism
Trying to heal people with medicines made from herbs.

Human sacrifice
Killing people as offerings to the gods.

Jade
A smooth, valuable, pale-green stone.

Loom
A frame fitted with threads, used for weaving cloth.

Mesoamerica
The region where North and South America meet. It includes the countries of Mexico, Honduras, Guatemala, Belize and El Salvador.

Mixtecs
A Mesoamerican people who lived in southern Mexico before the Aztecs.

Obsidian
A glassy black stone, produced when volcanoes erupt.

Shrine
A holy place, often containing the statue of a god.

Slaves
Men, women and children who were not free, but belonged to their owners. They could be bought and sold. Some were treated well, while others were treated badly.

Tortillas
Flat, crispy maize pancakes.

Tribute
Valuable goods given regularly to the Aztecs by cities and peoples they had conquered.

Turquoise
A beautiful, semi-precious blue-green stone.

Vigil
A time of watching and waiting.

▶ *An Aztec farmer harvesting amaranth. Its seeds were dried and then stewed to make porridge.*

AZTEC PROJECTS

If you want to find out more about the Aztecs, here are some ideas for projects.

MAKE A 'FEATHER' HEADDRESS
Aztec people wore wonderful headdresses, made of brightly coloured feathers from tropical birds. The bigger the headdress, the more important the wearer!

You will need:
sheets of coloured paper; a pen or pencil; scissors; a wide plastic headband or a piece of ribbon (about 2.5 cm wide), long enough to fit comfortably around your head with enough left over to tie in a bow; some plastic 'jewels' or gold-coloured paper; glue suitable to use on fabric.

1. Draw lots of feather shapes (at least 20), about 20 cm long, on coloured paper. Cut them out and cut fringes at the top end of each one.
2. Stick the feathers on to your headband or ribbon.
3. Decorate the feathers with plastic jewels or shapes cut from gold paper.
4. Put on your headband or tie the ribbon under your chin.

There are codex pictures of Aztecs wearing headdresses. The feathers did not stand up vertically but stuck out backwards, behind the wearer's head.

◄ *A reconstruction of an Aztec feather headdress.*

30

MAKE AN AZTEC-STYLE CHOCOLATE DRINK

People living in rainforests, who had been conquered by the Aztecs, sent them tributes of cacao beans. Today, we use these beans to make chocolate, but the Aztecs made them into a drink. They were so valuable that the Aztecs used them instead of money. They flavoured their chocolate with another American rainforest plant, vanilla.

You will need (makes 2 servings):

2 mugs milk; 100g chocolate (the darker the better) or 4 teaspoons pure cocoa powder; 4 teaspoons honey (more if you like things very sweet); 2 drops vanilla essence; a cheese grater; a saucepan.

(Ask an adult to help you with this recipe)

1. Grate the chocolate or mix the cocoa powder with a little milk to make a smooth runny paste.
2. Heat the milk in a saucepan.
3. When it is hot but NOT boiling, add the honey, grated chocolate or cocoa powder mix and vanilla. Stir.
4. Keep on stirring until the honey and the chocolate or cocoa powder have dissolved.
5. Bring very gently to the boil, stirring all the time, then remove from the heat straight away and pour into two mugs.

LEARN SOME AZTEC PICTURE WORDS

The Aztecs used glyphs, or pictures that stood for words, to record important events and to make lists of all the goods sent to them as tributes. This picture writing was very difficult to learn. Only priests or specially trained scribes could do it. Here are a few Aztec glyphs. Can you work out what they mean? (The answers are upside down at the bottom of page 32.)

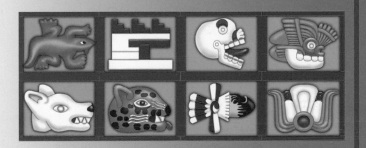

AZTECS ON THE INTERNET

Find out more about the Aztecs from these websites. Remember the Internet is constantly changing so if you can't find these websites, try searching using the word 'Aztecs'.

http://library.thinkquest.org/27981
This site has lots of useful links for pupils.

http://archaeology.la.asu.edu/tm/index2.php
This one includes a tour round the biggest Aztec museum in Mexico.

INDEX

ANSWERS TO GLYPHS QUIZ
Top row, left to right: lizard,
house, death's head, grass.
Bottom row, left to right: dog,
jaguar, flint knife, flower.